Paint a Sun in the Sky
A first look at the seasons

by Claire Llewellyn

MACDONALD YOUNG BOOKS

In spring, the first buds open on the trees.

Mmm! The weather's getting warmer. It must be spring.

6

And it's still light when we get home from school.

7

Spring blossom opens, and flowers

shoot up through the chilly ground.

9

In summer, the sun is high in the sky.

Out go thick jumpers and heavy coats.

In come sunhats,
T-shirts and shorts.

Flowerbeds and windowboxes buzz with bees.

Bees use nectar to make honey.

15

In early autumn, nuts, berries, apples

18

Soon, the leaves on the trees change colour

In winter, the sun is low in the sky.

The days are short and cold.

The best winter days have

bright sunshine and snow.

make up a picture of the year.

...a sun in the sky!

Why do we have seasons?

We have seasons because of the way the Earth moves around the Sun. This journey is called the Earth's orbit and it takes exactly one year.

1 In December, the South Pole leans towards the Sun. The south has summer. The north has winter.

The Earth isn't upright as it orbits the Sun. It's tilted to one side. So, at different times on its journey, first one pole and then the other leans towards the Sun. This is why we have seasons.

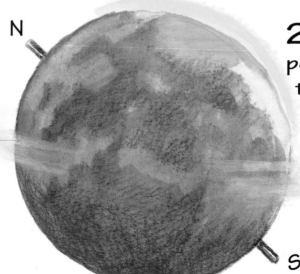

2 In March, neither pole leans towards the Sun, but the south is getting cooler (autumn) and the north is warming up (spring).